T0274407

*And out of the ground made the L*ORD *God to grow every tree that is pleasant to the sight, and good for food.*

—Genesis 2:9

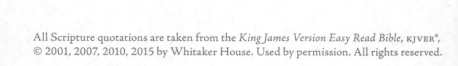

He is faithful that promised.   —Hebrews 10:23

For the eyes of the Lord are over the righteous,
and His ears are open to their prayers.
—1 Peter 3:12

The LORD has set apart him that is godly for Himself: the LORD will hear when I call to Him. —Psalm 4:3

And it shall come to pass, that before they call, I will answer;
and while they are yet speaking, I will hear.
—Isaiah 65:24

For whosoever shall call upon the name of the Lord shall be saved.
—Romans 10:13

If the Son therefore shall make you free, you shall be free indeed.
—John 8:36

_I, even I, am He that blots out your transgressions for My own sake,
and will not remember your sins._   —Isaiah 43:25

For the fruit of the Spirit is in all goodness and
righteousness and truth.
—Ephesians 5:9

The grass withers, the flower fades: but the word of our God shall stand for ever.   —Isaiah 40:8

But the Lord is faithful, who shall establish you,
and keep you from evil.
—2 Thessalonians 3:3

And He said, My presence shall go with you, and I will give you rest.
—Exodus 33:14

For where two or three are gathered together in My name,
there am I in the midst of them.
—Matthew 18:20

Lo, I am with you always, even to the end of the world.

—Matthew 28:20

As the Father has loved Me, so have I loved you:
continue you in My love.
—John 15:9

But God commends His love toward us, in that, while we were yet sinners, Christ died for us. —Romans 5:8

*You will keep him in perfect peace, whose mind is stayed on You:
because he trusts in You.*
—Isaiah 26:3

And the peace of God, which passes all understanding, shall keep your
hearts and minds through Christ Jesus.   —Philippians 4:7

For You are my hope, O LORD God: You are my trust from my youth.
—Psalm 71:5

_____

_____

_____

_____

_____

_____

_____

_____

_____

_____

_____

_____

_____

_____

_____

_____

_____

_____

_____

_____

For the wages of sin is death; but the gift of God is eternal life through Jesus Christ our Lord.   —Romans 6:23

When Christ, who is our life, shall appear,
then shall you also appear with Him in glory.
—Colossians 3:4

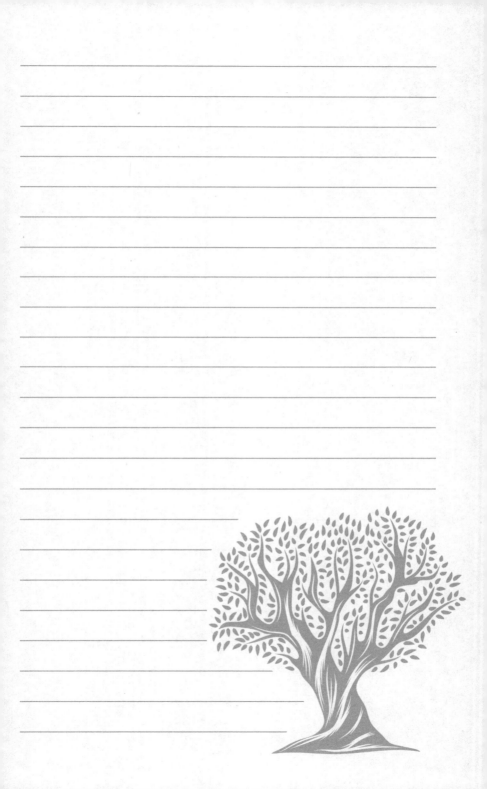

And Jesus said to him, Verily I say to you, Today shall you be with Me in paradise. —Luke 23:43

The LORD will give strength to His people;
the LORD will bless His people with peace.
—Psalm 29:11

Finally, my brethren, be strong in the Lord, and in the power of His might. —Ephesians 6:10

For God gives to a man that is good in His sight wisdom,
and knowledge, and joy.
—Ecclesiastes 2:26

_____

_____

_____

_____

_____

_____

_____

_____

_____

_____

_____

_____

_____

_____

_____

_____

_____

_____

_____

The fear of the Lord is the beginning of wisdom: and the knowledge of the holy is understanding. —Proverbs 9:10

I will bless the LORD, who has given me counsel:
my reins also instruct me in the night seasons.
—Psalm 16:7

I will instruct you and teach you in the way which you shall go: I will guide you with My eye. —Psalm 32:8

For this God is our God for ever and ever:
He will be our guide even to death.
—Psalm 48:14

_____

_____

_____

_____

_____

_____

_____

_____

_____

_____

_____

_____

_____

_____

_____

_____

_____

_____

_____

_____

In all your ways acknowledge Him, and He shall direct your paths.

—Proverbs 3:6

The fear of the LORD is the instruction of wisdom;
and before honor is humility.
—Proverbs 15:33

_____

_____

_____

_____

_____

_____

_____

_____

_____

_____

_____

_____

_____

_____

_____

_____

_____

_____

_____

_____

_____

_____

_____

_____

_____

_____

_____

_____

_____

_____

_____

_____

_____

_____

_____

_____

_____

_____

_____

_____

_____

_____

[The Lord] *satisfies your mouth with good things; so that your youth is renewed like the eagle's.* —Psalm 103:5

In the multitude of my thoughts within me
Your comforts delight my soul.
—Psalm 94:19

_____

_____

_____

_____

_____

_____

_____

_____

_____

_____

_____

_____

_____

_____

_____

_____

_____

Delight yourself also in the LORD; _and He shall give you the desires of your heart._   —Psalm 37:4

You open Your hand, and satisfy the desire of every living thing.
—Psalm 145:16

Train up a child in the way he should go: and when he is old, he will not depart from it. —Proverbs 22:6

For I will restore health to you,
and I will heal you of your wounds, says the LORD.
—Jeremiah 30:17

_____

_____

_____

_____

_____

_____

_____

_____

_____

_____

_____

_____

_____

_____

_____

_____

_____

_____

_____

_____

I am the LORD that heals you.   —Exodus 15:26

The fear of man brings a snare:
but whoso puts his trust in the LORD shall be safe.
—Proverbs 29:25

_____

_____

_____

_____

_____

_____

_____

_____

_____

_____

_____

_____

_____

_____

_____

_____

_____

_____

_____

He will keep the feet of His saints, and the wicked shall be silent in darkness; for by strength shall no man prevail. —1 Samuel 2:9

The fear of the Lord prolongs days:
but the years of the wicked shall be shortened.
—Proverbs 10:27

By humility and the fear of the Lord are riches, and honor, and life.
—Proverbs 22:4

But seek you first the kingdom of God, and His righteousness;
and all these things shall be added to you.
—Matthew 6:33

Believe in the LORD *your God, so shall you be established; believe His prophets, so shall you prosper.* —2 Chronicles 20:20

I have been young, and now am old;
yet have I not seen the righteous forsaken, nor his seed begging bread.
—Psalm 37:25

He causes the grass to grow for the cattle, and herb for the service of man: that he may bring forth food out of the earth. —Psalm 104:14

For I the LORD *your God will hold your right hand,*
saying to you, Fear not; I will help you.
—Isaiah 41:13

_____

_____

_____

_____

_____

_____

_____

_____

_____

_____

_____

_____

_____

_____

_____

_____

_____

_____

God has not given us the spirit of fear; but of power, and of love, and of a sound mind. —2 Timothy 1:7

Let not your heart be troubled: you believe in God, believe also in Me.
—John 14:1

_____

_____

_____

_____

_____

_____

_____

_____

_____

_____

_____

_____

_____

_____

_____

_____

_____

_____

Weeping may endure for a night, but joy comes in the morning.
—Psalm 30:5

God is not the author of confusion, but of peace.
—1 Corinthians 14:33

_____

_____

_____

_____

_____

_____

_____

_____

_____

_____

_____

_____

_____

_____

_____

_____

_____

_____

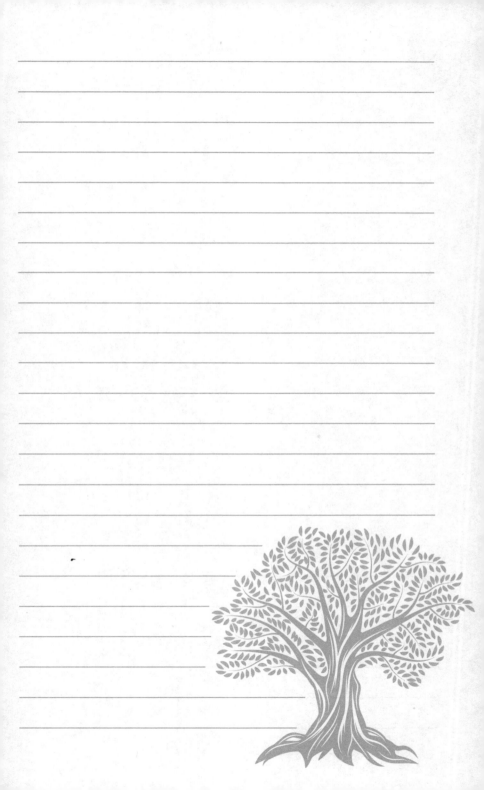

My flesh and my heart fails: but God is the strength of my heart, and
my portion for ever.   —Psalm 73:26

Be of good courage, and He shall strengthen your heart,
all you that hope in the LORD.
—Psalm 31:24

Trust in Him at all times; you people, pour out your heart before Him:
God is a refuge for us. —Psalm 62:8

And they that know Your name will put their trust in You:
*for You, L**ORD**, have not forsaken them that seek you.*
—Psalm 9:10

All have sinned, and come short of the glory of God; Being justified freely by His grace through the redemption that is in Christ Jesus.

—Romans 3:23–24

You have seen it; for You behold mischief and spite...
You are the helper of the fatherless.
—Psalm 10:14

_____

_____

_____

_____

_____

_____

_____

_____

_____

_____

_____

_____

_____

_____

_____

_____

_____

_____

_____

So that we may boldly say, The Lord is my helper, and I will not fear what man shall do to me. —Hebrews 13:6

The trying of your faith works patience. But let patience have her perfect work, that you may be perfect and entire, wanting nothing.
—James 1:3–4

_____

_____

_____

_____

_____

_____

_____

_____

_____

_____

_____

_____

_____

_____

_____

_____

_____

_____

_____

When my father and my mother forsake me, then the Lord will take me up. —Psalm 27:10

Humble yourselves therefore under the mighty hand of God,
that He may exalt you in due time: Casting all your care upon Him;
for He cares for you.
—1 Peter 5:6–7

All things are possible to him that believes.   —Mark 9:23

Be strong and of a good courage; be not afraid, neither be
you dismayed: for the LORD your God is with you wherever you go.
—Joshua 1:9

These things I have spoken to you, that in Me you might have peace. In the world you shall have tribulation: but be of good cheer; I have over-come the world. —John 16:33

Blessed is the man that endures temptation:
for when he is tried, he shall receive the crown of life, which the Lord
has promised to them that love Him.
—James 1:12

Submit yourselves therefore to God. Resist the devil, and he will flee from you.
             —James 4:7

The God of peace shall bruise Satan under your feet shortly.
The grace of our Lord Jesus Christ be with you.
—Romans 16:20

_We glory in tribulations also: knowing that tribulation works pa-
tience._   —Romans 5:3

I will take sickness away from the midst of you.
—Exodus 23:25

The LORD has comforted His people, and will have mercy upon His afflicted. —Isaiah 49:13

I have blotted out, as a thick cloud, your transgressions, and, as a cloud, your sins: return to Me; for I have redeemed you.
—Isaiah 44:22

_____

_____

_____

_____

_____

_____

_____

_____

_____

_____

_____

_____

_____

_____

_____

_____

_____

_____

_____

Let all those that put their trust in You rejoice: let them ever shout for joy, because You defend them. —Psalm 5:11

Blessed are they which are persecuted for righteousness' sake:
for theirs is the kingdom of heaven.
—Matthew 5:10

_____

_____

_____

_____

_____

_____

_____

_____

_____

_____

_____

_____

_____

_____

_____

_____

_____

_____

_____

_____

_____

If we believe not, yet He abides faithful: He cannot deny Himself.
—2 Timothy 2:13

Whosoever shall do the will of My Father which is in heaven,
the same is My brother, and sister, and mother.
—Matthew 12:50

Blessed are they that hear the word of God, and keep it.

—Luke 11:28

Blessed is that man that makes the LORD his trust, and respects not
the proud, nor such as turn aside to lies.
—Psalm 40:4

Our heart shall rejoice in Him, because we have trusted in His holy name. Let Your mercy, O LORD, be upon us, according as we hope in You. —Psalm 33:21–22

And you shall seek Me, and find Me, when you shall search for Me
with all your heart. And I will be found of you, says the LORD.
—Jeremiah 29:13–14

Let all those that seek You rejoice and be glad in You. —Psalm 70:4

The LORD preserves all them that love Him:
but all the wicked will He destroy.
—Psalm 145:20

Whosoever lives and believes in Me shall never die.   —John 11:26

The angel of the LORD encamps round about them that fear Him,
and delivers them.
—Psalm 34:7

The effectual fervent prayer of a righteous man avails much.

—James 5:16

Blessed is he that considers the poor:
the LORD will deliver him in time of trouble.
—Psalm 41:1

Remember the words of the Lord Jesus, how He said, It is more blessed
to give than to receive. —Acts 20:35

As you are partakers of the sufferings,
so shall you be also of the consolation.
—2 Corinthians 1:7

The righteous cry, and the LORD hears, and delivers them out of all their troubles. —Psalm 34:17

Then shall the righteous shine forth as the sun in the kingdom of their Father.
—Matthew 13:43

When a man's ways please the Lord, He makes even his enemies to be at peace with him. —Proverbs 16:7

Study to show yourself approved to God,
a workman that needs not to be ashamed.
—2 Timothy 2:15

He that walks uprightly walks surely: but he that perverts his ways shall be known. —Proverbs 10:9

A faithful man shall abound with blessings: but he that makes haste to be rich shall not be innocent.
—Proverbs 28:20

Be you faithful to death, and I will give you a crown of life.
—Revelation 2:10

*He that is faithful in that which is least is faithful also in much: and he
that is unjust in the least is unjust also in much.*
—Luke 16:10

The lip of truth shall be established for ever: but a lying tongue is but for a moment. —Proverbs 12:19

The thoughts of the diligent tend only to plenteousness.
—Proverbs 21:5

For You, Lord, will bless the righteous; with favor will
You compass him as with a shield.
—Psalm 5:12

If you be reproached for the name of Christ, happy are you; for the Spirit of glory and of God rests upon you. —1 Peter 4:14

When you do well, and suffer for it, you take it patiently,
this is acceptable with God.
—1 Peter 2:20

_____

_____

_____

_____

_____

_____

_____

_____

_____

_____

_____

_____

_____

_____

_____

_____

_____

_____

_____

He that gives to the poor shall not lack. —Proverbs 28:27

Let us not be weary in well doing:
for in due season we shall reap, if we faint not.
—Galatians 6:9

[Build] up yourselves on your most holy faith, praying in the Holy Ghost.   —Jude 20

Who is he that overcomes the world,
but he that believes that Jesus is the Son of God?
—1 John 5:5